D0931003

# Wacky
# HOCKEY
# TRIVIA

## Fun Facts for Every Fan

By Shane Frederick

CAPSTONE PRESS
a capstone imprint

Sports Illustrated Kids Wacky Sports Trivia is published by Capstone Press,
1710 Roe Crest Drive, North Mankato, Minnesota 56003.
www.mycapstone.com

**Library of Congress Cataloging-in-Publication Data**
Names: Frederick, Shane.
Title: Wacky hockey trivia : fun facts for every fan / by Shane Frederick.
Description: North Mankato, Minnesota : An imprint of Capstone Press, [2017]
  | Series: Sports Illustrated Kids. Wacky Sports Trivia | Includes
  bibliographical references, webography and index. | Audience: Ages: 9-15.?
  | Audience: Grades: 4 to 6.?
Identifiers: LCCN 2016010278|
ISBN 9781515719915 (library binding) |
ISBN 9781515720010 (eBook PDF)
Subjects: LCSH: Hockey—Miscellanea—Juvenile literature.
Classification: LCC GV847.25 .F75 2017 | DDC 796.962—dc23
LC record available at http://lccn.loc.gov/2016010278

**Editorial Credits**
Brenda Haugen, editor; Terri Poburka, designer; Eric Gohl, media researcher;
Tori Abraham, production specialist

**Photo Credits**
AP Photo: 29, Joe Giza, 9; Getty Images: B Bennett, 6, 8, 13 (Vezina), 21, 23, John Preito, 10;
Newscom: Cal Sport Media/Aaron Doster, 22 (hat trick), Everett Collection, 25, Icon SMI/
IHA, 7, 15, iPhoto Inc./Dave Abel, 18, Reuters/Mike Cassese, 16, Reuters/Shaun Best,
27; Shutterstock: Alexlukin, 13 (pickle), Andrey Lobachev, 11 (dollar bill), GrandeDuc,
cover, background (throughout), Moolkum, 22 (cap), picturepartners, 20, (octopus), Pond
Thananat, (bottle); Sports Illustrated: David E. Klutho, 5, 11 (Draper), 19, 20 (bottom), 24,
28, Heinz Kluetmeier, 17, Hy Peskin, 12, Tony Triolo, 4, 14, 26

Printed in the United States of America.
032016      009682F16

# Table of Contents

# A FAST AND FUNNY GAME

Did you know that the fastest goal at the beginning of a National Hockey League (NHL) game came just 5 seconds after the opening **face-off**? That barely gave people enough time to sit down and take a bite of their popcorn.

For the people who did see the goal, it's something they will probably never forget. But it has happened more than once. NHLers Doug Smail, Bryan Trottier, and Alexander Mogilny are all tied for that record.

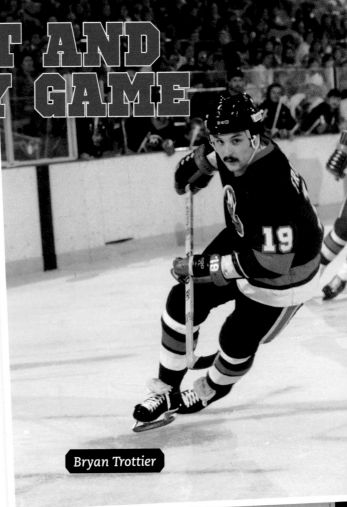

Bryan Trottier

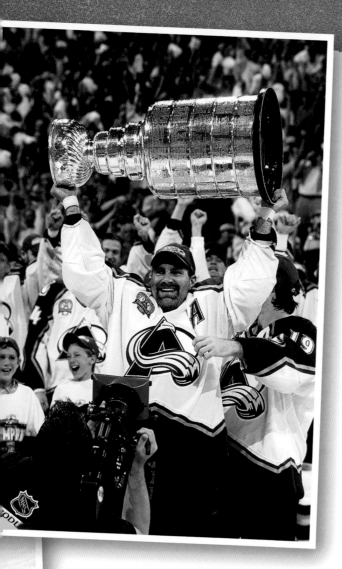

The sport of hockey is full of amazing plays and personalities, remarkable records and feats, and surprising stories and accomplishments. Who spent three days in the **penalty box**? Who lost the **Stanley Cup**—not the championship series but the actual cup? And who is the Chicoutimi Cucumber? The answers to those questions are part of the wacky story of hockey.

**face-off**—when a player from each team battles for possession of the puck to start or restart play

**penalty box**—the place where a player serves time for breaking the rules of the game

**Stanley Cup**—the trophy given each year to the NHL champion

# Chapter 1

# COLORFUL CHARACTERS

A hockey team plays with six players on the ice and several more on the bench ready to get in the game. There are superstars and grinders, goalies, and goons. Some just go work every night and do their job. Others have shaped the way the game is played.

## "BOOM BOOM" MAKES A NOISE
★ ★ ★

Bernie Geoffrion is credited with inventing the **slap shot**, the hardest, fastest shot in hockey. If he wasn't the first to do it, he was the first to perfect it, playing for the Montreal Canadiens in the 1950s and 1960s. The explosive noise made when Geoffrion took the shot, along with the one it made when it missed the net and hit the boards, gave Geoffrion his nickname, "Boom Boom."

Bernie Geoffrion

### ★★★ GIRL POWER ★★★

In the fall of 1992, Manon Rhéaume became the first and only woman to play an NHL game. Rhéaume, a goaltender, was invited to join the Tampa Bay Lightning in training camp. She played between the posts for one period of an **exhibition** game against the St. Louis Blues. She allowed two goals and made seven saves. While she didn't get a spot on the Lightning roster, Rhéaume did play against the men in the minor leagues for four seasons.

Manon Rhéaume

**slap shot**—the fastest and most forceful shot in the game; a player raises his or her stick and slaps the puck hard toward the goal, putting his or her full body power behind it

**exhibition**—a game played only for show

Dave "Tiger" Williams (22)

### ★★★ CAGED TIGER ★★★

Dave "Tiger" Williams spent a total of more than three days in the penalty box—not all at once though. Playing for five teams over 14 seasons, Williams racked up more penalty minutes than any other player. His total included 3,966 minutes during the regular season and another 455 minutes during playoff games. Williams was an enforcer whose role was to protect his team's star players. However, he first got his tough-guy nickname, Tiger, when he was just 5 years old.

## ★★★ TAKE A SEAT ★★★

Chris "Knuckles" Nilan of the Montreal Canadiens, Boston Bruins, and New York Rangers was known for his willingness to fight. He was penalized 10 times for 42 minutes in a single game. That's more than two periods in the penalty box.

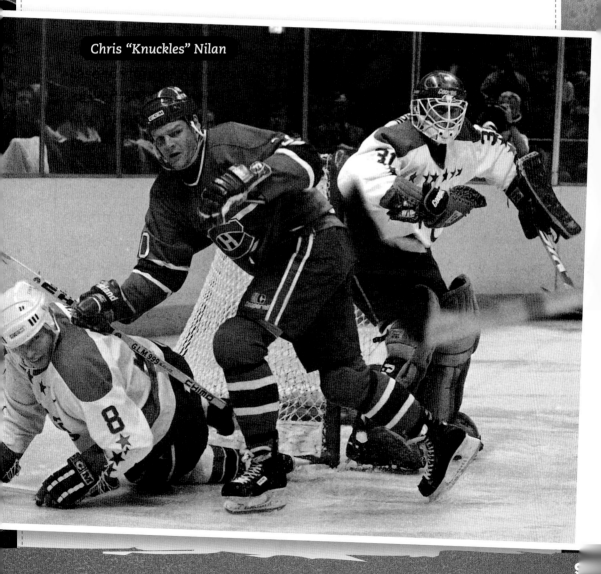

Chris "Knuckles" Nilan

Randy Pierce (7)

### ★★★ PUCKER UP ★★★

Randy Pierce of the Colorado Rockies received one of the most unusual penalties in NHL history. During a game in 1979 against the New York Islanders, Pierce scored a late goal into an empty net. Thinking he just ensured his team's first-ever victory over the Islanders, Pierce celebrated by picking up the puck, kissing it, and tossing it into the stands. That was a no-no. The referee put Pierce in the penalty box for delay of game. Fortunately for Pierce, the Rockies hung on to win the game.

# ★★★ WHAT A BARGAIN! ★★★

Kris Draper was one of the best bargains in NHL history. He played in more than 1,000 games for the Detroit Red Wings and helped them win four Stanley Cups. All the Red Wings had to give up for him in a trade with the Winnipeg Jets was one dollar, which earned Draper the nickname the "One Dollar Man."

Kris Draper

### ★★★ NAME GAME ★★★

Maurice Richard was known as "Rocket" because of his blazing speed as a skater for the Montreal Canadiens. His teammate and younger brother, Henri, who was 3 inches (7.6 centimeters) shorter than Maurice, was nicknamed "Pocket Rocket."

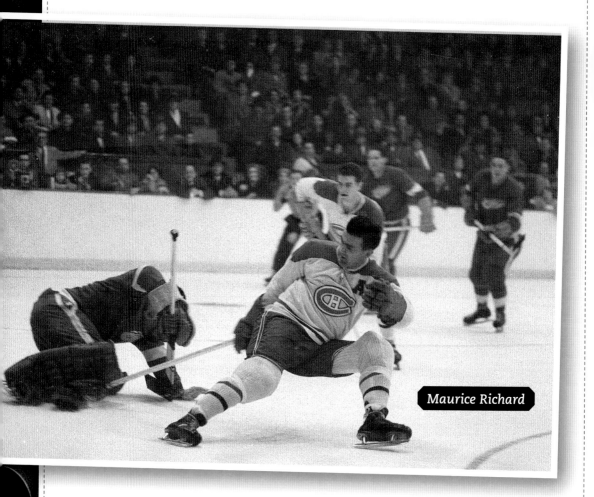

Maurice Richard

## WHAT'S IN A NICKNAME?

★ ★ ★

Hockey players love to use nicknames. One of the strangest nicknames belonged to Georges Vezina, the man whose name is on the trophy that goes to the best goaltender each season. Vezina was known as the "Chicoutimi Cucumber" because he was from Chicoutimi, Quebec, and remained "cool as a cucumber" when he played.

Georges Vezina

# Chapter 2

# SUPERSTITIONS AND SURPRISES

Many people live with **superstitions**. Some wear a pair of lucky socks. Some follow the same routine before taking a test. Hockey players are no different. Plenty of hockey players believe they can add a little bit of good luck to their games by doing some pretty strange things.

### A LOT OF LACES
★ ★ ★

Ray Bourque

Ray Bourque was a superstitious player. The **defenseman** for the Boston Bruins and Colorado Avalanche changed the laces of his skates between every period and after every game. The fresh laces, he believed, improved his game. Doing the math, Bourque, who played in 1,826 games, went through more than 5,000 pairs of laces!

### ★★★ IRON MAN ★★★

Goaltending is a tough job. Nowadays even the best goalies need a day off. That wasn't the case for Glenn Hall, though. In the 1950s and 1960s, he played 502 consecutive complete games, as well as 49 playoff games, for the Detroit Red Wings and Chicago Blackhawks. It's a record for goalies that likely will never be broken. Hall got so excited before every game that he usually would throw up. Then he'd drink some orange juice and be ready to head out to the ice. Hall's playing streak finally came to an end when he hurt his back while bending over to fix a toe strap.

Glenn Hall

**superstition**—a belief that an action can affect the outcome of a future event

**defenseman**—a player whose main job is to prevent opponents from getting open shots on goal

### ★★★ MAGIC POWDER ★★★

Joe Nieuwendyk sprinkled baby powder on the blades of his hockey sticks before every game. He thought the powder had magical powers to help him score goals. He might have been right. In his 20 NHL seasons, he scored 564 career goals.

Joe Nieuwendyk

Patrick Roy

### ★★★ TALK TO THE GOAL ★★★

**Hall of Fame** goaltender Patrick Roy of the Montreal Canadiens and Colorado Avalanche had some unusual buddies on the ice. Roy admitted that he talked to his goal posts during games. When asked after one game if the posts talked back, Roy said, "I guess so. They made two stops tonight."

**Hall of Fame**—a place where people important to the NHL are honored

### ★★★ MAN IN THE MASK ★★★

Goaltenders today have all kinds of unusual designs painted on their helmets. The first goalie masks, however, were quite plain. The Boston Bruins' Gerry Cheevers, one of the stars of the late-1960s and 1970s, decided to show everyone just how important his face protection was. Every time a puck hit his mask, he drew stitches on it, marking the spot where he probably would have been cut and sewn up. Eventually the mask was almost completely covered with black stitch marks.

Gerry Cheevers

Mario Lemieux

### ★★★ IT'S HIS TEAM ★★★

Mario Lemieux was the first team owner to also play for his club. One of the NHL's all-time greats, Lemieux battled cancer and back problems before he chose to retire in 1997. A few months later, he was inducted into the Hockey Hall of Fame. Two years after that, Lemieux bought a share of the Penguins. In 2000 Lemieux decided he wanted to return to the ice. He played parts of five more seasons before retiring again for good.

# chapter 3

# WACKY TRADITIONS

**Tradition** is important in the game of hockey. For instance, each team's starting goalie gets to step on the ice first, and every playoff series ends in a respectful handshake line between the two teams. But there are some strange traditions too, including a few involving fans throwing things onto the ice.

### ★★★ WINGS GET SLIMED ★★★

There are few traditions like the one at playoff time in Detroit when an octopus is thrown onto the ice during each game. The custom began in 1952. Brothers Pete and Jerry Cusimano brought one of the sea creatures to Olympia Stadium. Why an octopus? The slimy creature's eight legs represented, at the time, the number of wins a team needed to capture the Stanley Cup. In 1996 a massive, 50-pound (22.7-kilogram) octopus was thrown onto the ice and was later paraded around the rink on the hood of the Zamboni.

### ★★★ RAT TRICK ★★★

Can a rodent be a good-luck charm? The Florida Panthers think so. Early in the 1995–96 season, the Panthers' Scott Mellanby used his stick to kill a rat in the locker room. Mellanby went on to score two goals using that stick in the following game. His teammate, John Vanbiesbrouck called it a "rat trick." The fans caught on, tossing plastic rats on the ice after Panther goals. One night that season, during the team's run to the Stanley Cup Finals, nearly 3,000 rats were tossed on the ice.

**tradition**—customs, ideas, or beliefs passed down through time

### ★★★ TIP OF THE HAT ★★★

The term **hat trick** goes back to the 1850s and the game of cricket. But it later gained ground in the hockey world. In 1946 the Chicago Blackhawks' Alex Kaleta visited a store before a game in Toronto and had his eye on a particular hat. The owner said he'd give it to him for free, but there was a catch: Kaleta needed to score three goals in that night's game. Kaleta scored four! The owner gave him the hat and then began giving hats to other players who had three-goal games for or against the Toronto Maple Leafs. Nowadays fans throw hats on the ice when a player gets a hat trick.

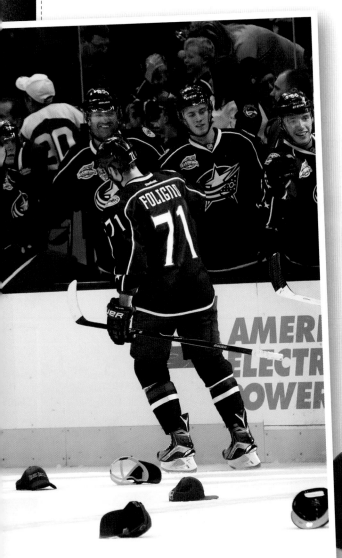

Bill Mosienko

### ★★★ SPEEDY SCORER ★★★

Bill Mosienko of the Chicago Blackhawks recorded the fastest hat trick in NHL history. On the final day of the 1952 regular season, he scored three goals in a span of just 21 seconds! Teammate Gus Bodnar lent a hand in all three goals, meaning he has the record for the NHL's fastest three **assists**.

**hat trick**—when a player scores three goals in one game

**assist**—a pass that leads to a score by a teammate

### ★★★ LORD STANLEY IS LOST! ★★★

The winner of the NHL championship each year receives the Stanley Cup as a prize. Following the playoffs, each member of the winning team gets to spend a day with the trophy. It's been taken all over the world. Players have eaten out of it, drank out of it, and even bathed babies in it. In 1907, in the days before the NHL was formed, a team called the Montreal Wanderers won the Stanley Cup—and then promptly lost it! It was missing for months before they realized they had left it at a photography studio where they'd had a team picture taken with it. The photographer's mother had turned the silver trophy into a flowerpot.

## ★★★ GAME OVER ★★★

The Stanley Cup is the oldest trophy in professional sports and has been hockey's biggest prize since 1893. There have been two years in which it was not awarded. In 2005 the NHL season was canceled due to a dispute between the team owners and players. In 1919 a worldwide flu outbreak wiped out the finals. That year a matchup between the NHL-champion Montreal Canadiens and the Seattle Metropolitans of the Pacific Coast Hockey Association was going to decide the Stanley Cup winner. Five games in, with each team having won two games and another ending in a tie, several members of the Canadiens fell ill. The series was canceled. The names of both teams are engraved on the Cup.

# INFLUENZA

## FREQUENTLY COMPLICATED WITH

# PNEUMONIA

### IS PREVALENT AT THIS TIME THROUGHOUT AMERICA.

### THIS THEATRE IS CO-OPERATING WITH THE DEPARTMENT OF HEALTH.

## YOU MUST DO THE SAME

### IF YOU HAVE A COLD AND ARE COUGHING AND SNEEZING. DO NOT ENTER THIS THEATRE

## GO HOME AND GO TO BED UNTIL YOU ARE WELL

Coughing, Sneezing or Spitting Will Not Be Permitted In The Theatre. In case you must cough or Sneeze, do so in your own hand-kerchief, and if the Coughing or Sneezing Persists Leave The Theatre At Once.

This Theatre has agreed to co-operate with the Department Of Health in disseminating the truth about Influenza, and thus serve a great educational purpose.

## HELP US TO KEEP CHICAGO THE HEALTHIEST CITY IN THE WORLD

### JOHN DILL ROBERTSON

#### COMMISSIONER OF HEALTH

# Chapter 4

# TOTALLY EXTREME

One of the most exciting things about being a sports fan is the possibility of seeing a rare feat or even something that hasn't been done before. Seeing a special play— or a special player—sticks in a fan's memory forever.

## THE GREAT ONE
★ ★ ★

Hockey's best player, Wayne Gretzky, holds so many NHL records that he holds the record for the most records—61. Known as "The Great One," Gretzky ranks as the NHL's all-time leading scorer—and by a long shot. During his career, he collected 2,857 **points**. If you took away all of his goals, he'd still hold the career points record on assists alone with 1,963.

Wayne Gretzky

## ★★★ GOAL-SCORER'S DREAM ★★★

On its way to qualifying for the 2010 Olympics, the Slovakian women's hockey team defeated Bulgaria 82–0. The team averaged one goal every 44 seconds. One player scored 10 times! Once it reached the Olympics, however, Slovakia was on the other end of a lopsided score and lost to Canada 18–0.

**points**—a player's total number of goals and assists

## GOAL-SCORING GOALIES
★ ★ ★

The goaltender's job is to stop the puck. But six NHL goalies have scored goals by shooting the puck into an open net at the other end of the rink. The group includes Ron Hextall, Chris Osgood, Martin Brodeur, Jose Theodore, Evgeni Nabokov, and Mike Smith. Hextall, of the Philadelphia Flyers, was the first goalie to shoot and score, accomplishing the feat on December 8, 1987. A season later, in the playoffs, he did it again. Brodeur was also credited for a second goal but only because he was the last player to touch the puck before an opposing player put the puck in his own net.

## A LONG NIGHT
★★★

The longest NHL game took place on March 24, 1936. It was a playoff game between Detroit Red Wings and

Detroit manager Jack Adams hugged Johnny Sorrell (left) and Scotty Bowman after the Red Wings won the 1936 NHL championship.

the Montreal Maroons. It took six overtimes before the Red Wings' Mud Bruneteau finally scored, giving his team a 1–0 victory. The teams played 176 minutes, 30 seconds of hockey, but in real time it lasted much longer—nearly six hours. The game started at 8:30 p.m. and finally ended at 2:25 a.m.

## ★★★ A WILD AND WACKY GAME ★★★

In the whirlwind of all that happens on the ice during a hockey game or a hockey season, you might not think there's much time for trivial matters. But the sport is full of unpredictable and crazy plays, amazing and unbelievable players, and strange and—yes—wacky characters to cheer for every single night. It's still astonishing that Wayne Gretzky set up more goals than any other player has ever scored or that a team once won a game 82–0. Besides the thrill of the game, those are some of the reasons people love hockey and the NHL, and why they keep coming back to watch.

# ★ Glossary ★

**assist** (uh-SIST)—a pass that leads to a score by a teammate

**defenseman** (di-FENS-muhn)—a player whose main job is to prevent opponents from getting open shots on goal

**exhibition** (ek-suh-BI-shuhn)—a game played only for show

**face-off** (FAYSS-awf)—when a player from each team battles for possession of the puck to start or restart play

**Hall of Fame** (HOL UV FAYM)—a place where people important to the NHL are honored

**hat trick** (HAT TRIK)—when a player scores three goals in one game

**penalty box** (PEN-uhl-tee BAHKSS)—the place where a player serves time for breaking the rules of the game

**points** (POYNTZ)—a player's total number of goals and assists

**slap shot** (SLAP SHAHT)—the fastest and most forceful shot in the game; a player raises his or her stick and slaps the puck hard toward the goal, putting his or her full body power behind it

**Stanley Cup** (STAN-lee KUP)—the trophy given each year to the NHL champion

**superstition** (soo-pur-STI-shuhn)—a belief that an action can affect the outcome of a future event

**tradition** (truh-DISH-uhn)—customs, ideas, or beliefs passed down through time

# ★ Read More ★

**Frederick, Shane.** *Hockey Stats and the Stories Behind Them: What Every Fan Needs to Know.* Sports Illustrated Kids: Sports Stats and Stories. North Mankato: Capstone Press, 2016.

**Herman, Gail.** *Who Is Wayne Gretzky?* Who Was ...? New York: Grosset & Dunlap, 2015.

**Myers, Dan.** *Hockey Trivia.* Sports Trivia. Minneapolis: Abdo Pub., 2016.

# ★ Internet Sites ★

FactHound offers a safe, fun way to find Internet sites related to this book. All of the sites on FactHound have been researched by our staff.

Here's all you do:

Visit *www.facthound.com*

Type in this code: 9781515719915

Check out projects, games and lots more at
**www.capstonekids.com**

# ★ Index ★